THE HAPPINESS MYTH

BREAKING FREE

TRACEY ARCHAMBEAULT

All client stories are composite examples drawn from common coaching experiences. Names and specific details have been changed to protect privacy.

FOREWORD

Dear Reader,

Have you ever found yourself wondering, "Is this it? Is this the happiness I've been working so hard for?" If so, you're not alone. "The Happiness Myth: Breaking Free" is a voyage into the heart of these questions, a journey I am excited to share with you.

As a life coach who has danced through the glittering illusions of the entertainment world, I've learned that true happiness isn't found under the bright lights or at the end of a roaring applause. Instead, it's nestled in the quieter moments, often hidden by the roles we play and the masks we wear. This book peels back those layers, challenging the myths that bind us to fleeting joys and external validations.

Each chapter in this book draws on both my personal experiences and professional insights to debunk widespread beliefs about happiness. We'll explore why the chase for external achievements, from the perfect job to the dream house, often leads us back to where we started, searching for something more.

But this isn't just a book about the myths of happiness; it's a guide to finding lasting joy. Through real-life scenarios, practical exercises, and engaging stories, we'll navigate the complex terrains of emotional well, being together. I'll share not only the struggles and setbacks of my own journey but also the breakthroughs that have transformed my understanding of what it means to truly live.

So, whether you're feeling stuck on the hamster wheel of life, looking to connect your heart and brain, or simply curious about a different perspective on happiness, I invite you to dive into these pages. Let's challenge the status quo together and discover the enduring joy that lies in authenticity, emotional intelligence, and the courage to embrace life as it is.

Thank you for joining me on this transformative journey. Here's to finding happiness, not as a distant goal, but as a present reality.

Warmly,

Tracey Archambeault

CONTENTS

INTRODUCTION: THE JOURNEY TO TRUE HAPPINESS BEGINS

INTRODUCTION

Welcome to "The Happiness Myth: Breaking Free" a journey into the heart (what happiness truly means and how we often misconstrue it with fleetin shadows of joy. In this book, we embark on a quest to dismantle the myth that have long dictated our pursuit of happiness, urging us to look inward an redefine our understanding of fulfillment.

Happiness. This word conjures images of blissful moments, achievement and acquisitions that society tells us are the benchmarks of a successful lif From childhood, we're taught to chase after these markers: the high-payin job, the perfect relationship, the dream home. Yet, so often, when we gras these things, we find ourselves holding not the key to lasting contentmen but rather a temporary ticket to satisfaction.

Why is our happiness so transient? Why does it feel like no achievement (purchase can satisfy us for long? These are the questions that drove me t write this book. As a life coach and someone who has navigated the sparklin yet superficial seas of the entertainment industry, I've seen firsthand how th glitz and glamour can fade, leaving behind a yearning for something deepe and more enduring.

In "The Happiness Myth: Breaking Free" we will explore how happiness is n(a commodity to be won or a territory to be conquered. Instead, it is a stat of being that flourishes from within when we learn to disconnect our sens of joy from the external world and its unpredictable waves. Through person anecdotes, cutting-edge research, and practical exercises, we will peel bac the layers of misconceptions and reveal the core principles of true happines

This book is divided into chapters that each tackle a specific myth about happiness, from the belief that happiness is something we can buy or achieve, to the notion that it always lies just beyond the next milestone. As we debunk these myths, I invite you to engage actively with the exercises and reflections provided, to not just read about happiness, but to start experiencing it in real-time, in your own life.

My goal is for you to close this book not only better informed about what happiness isn't but also empowered with the knowledge and tools to cultivate the happiness that has always been possible within you. Let us journey together from illusion to enlightenment, from fleeting pleasures to lasting joy. Welcome to a new understanding of happiness—one that is not chased, but rather, cultivated and cherished.

CHAPTER ONE

BREAKING FREE FROM EXTERNAL VALIDATION

Have you ever achieved something you've wanted for years, only to find yourself asking, "Is this all there is?" Before we explore this question together, let's take a moment to reflect on where you are in your own journey with happiness and achievement.

Think about your most recent accomplishment. Perhaps it was a career milestone, a personal goal, or a long-awaited purchase. How did you feel in that moment of achievement? More importantly, how do you feel about it now? Take a moment to write down your thoughts - this reflection will be valuable as we move forward.

THE SCIENCE OF ACHIEVEMENT AND HAPPINESS

Recent research in positive psychology helps us understand why achievements often don't bring the lasting happiness we expect. Dr. Sonja Lyubomirsky's studies at the University of California reveal that external circumstances, including our achievements and possessions, account for only 10% of our overall happiness levels. This finding has been further supported by Dr. Martin Seligman's work at the University of Pennsylvania, which demonstrates that authentic happiness stems more from engaging our personal strengths and finding meaning than from external achievements.

Take a moment to consider: What percentage of your happiness do you believe comes from external achievements? How does this compare to the research findings?

This pattern appears consistently across different life experiences. Consider these stories from people who have grappled with the same challenge:

Sarah, a technology executive, recently achieved what she had considered her ultimate career goal.

> ***"When I finally made CTO, I thought everything would fall into place," she shared. "The title, the salary, the recognition – it was everything I'd been working .. But three months later, I found myself just as stressed as before, just at a higher level."***

Marcus, a visual artist, described feeling oddly empty after his first successful gallery showing:

> ***"Everyone was praising my work, but instead of feeling fulfilled, I felt almost hollow. The validation I got from others didn't fill the void I expected it to."***

Elena, a recent medical school graduate, found herself immediately shifting focus to the next challenge:

> ***"The moment I achieved my dream of graduating, I started worrying about residency. It's like the goalposts keep moving on their own."***

Pause for a moment and reflect: Which of these stories resonates most with your own experience? What patterns do you notice in how you respond to achievements?

UNDERSTANDING OUR PATTERNS

The cycle of achievement and temporary satisfaction follows a predictable pattern, one that psychologists call hedonic adaptation. This natural tendency to return to a baseline level of happiness despite major positive changes helps explain why even significant achievements don't permanently alter our happiness levels.

A 2022 study in the Journal of Positive Psychology found that individuals who focused on internal growth rather than external achievements reported significantly higher levels of sustained well-being. The research tracked participants over an 18-month period, revealing that those who developed strong internal validation practices showed a 40% increase in their baseline happiness levels.

Understanding these patterns creates a crucial turning point in our relationship with happiness. When we recognize that our pursuit of achievement-based happiness follows predictable cycles, we can begin to see beyond them. Like noticing that we're caught in a revolving door, this awareness presents us with a choice: we can continue spinning through the same patterns, or we can step onto a new path. This is where the journey of breaking free begins – not with a dramatic leap, but with small, intentional steps toward a different way of experiencing success and fulfillment.

BREAKING FREE: A NEW APPROACH

The journey from external validation to internal fulfillment isn't about giving up on achievements - it's about transforming your relationship with them. This transformation happens through three key stages that research has shown to be most effective.

Before we explore these stages, take a moment to consider: How would your approach to goals change if you were completely free from the need for others' approval?

The three key stages are:

1. First comes awareness: Simply noticing when you seek external approval creates space for change. Michael, a software developer, describes this first stage: "I started keeping track of how often I checked my performance metrics throughout the day. Just noticing this habit was eye-opening."
2. Next is understanding: Recognizing why we seek external validation helps us develop healthier patterns. Research shows that our drive for external validation often stems from early experiences and cultural conditioning. Understanding this can help reduce self-judgment as we work to create change.
3. Finally comes action: Small, consistent steps toward internal validation build a new foundation for happiness. Recent research by Dr. Kristin Neff at the University of Texas shows that practicing self-validation can significantly reduce anxiety and increase resilience, even in high-pressure environments.

COMMON CHALLENGES AND SOLUTIONS

Many people face specific challenges as they work to break free from external validation. Let's explore these challenges and see how others have successfully navigated them:

The Comparison Trap:

Jamie, a marketing professional, found herself constantly comparing her career progress to her peers' LinkedIn updates. Her solution? She created a "personal growth tracker" focusing solely on her own learning journey. "Instead of measuring myself against others," she explains, "I started asking myself what I learned each week. This simple shift changed everything."

Fear of Complacency:

David, an entrepreneur, worried that letting go of external validation would make him lose his edge. He discovered that connecting his work to his personal values actually increased his motivation. "When I started measuring success by how well I served my clients rather than by my revenue numbers," he shares, "I became more innovative and, ironically, more successful."

Cultural Pressure:

Mai, a first-generation professional, struggled with family expectations of traditional success markers. She found balance by creating her own definition of success while honoring her family's values. "I learned to translate my parents' wish for security into my own terms," she explains. "Now I can appreciate their concern while staying true to my own path."

As you read these examples, consider: Which challenge feels most relevant to your life? What strategy might you adapt to your own situation?

TAKING ACTION: YOUR NEXT STEPS

As we conclude this chapter, let's focus on concrete steps you can take today:

1. Start a validation journal. For one week, notice and record when you seek external approval. Look for patterns in your observations.
2. Practice internal validation. Each evening, acknowledge one thing you did well, regardless of whether anyone else noticed.
3. Develop your own success metrics. What would achievement look like if you were the only one keeping score?

Day	External Validation Sought	What I Did Well	Insight
Monday.			
Tuesday			
Wednesday			
Thursday			
Friday			
Saturday			
Sunday			

Before moving on, take a moment to reflect: What one small step could you take today toward more sustainable happiness?

LOOKING AHEAD

In our next chapter, we'll explore another pervasive myth: the belief that happiness lives in the future. But for now, take time to reflect on your relationship with external validation. Remember, this journey isn't about perfection – it's about progress. Each small step toward internal validation builds a stronger foundation for lasting joy.

CHAPTER

TWO

FINDING JOY IN THE NOW

Have you ever caught yourself saying, "I'll be happy when..."? Maybe you were sitting in traffic, thinking about how much better life will be after you move closer to work. Or perhaps you were scrolling through social media, imagining how content you'll feel once you achieve that perfect relationship, ideal body, or dream career. We've all been there – constantly pushing our happiness just beyond the horizon, always a few steps ahead of where we stand.

Let's pause for a moment and try something together. Think about the last time you achieved something you'd been looking forward to. Remember how you felt in that moment of accomplishment? Now, how long did that feeling last before your mind started reaching for the next milestone? This pattern is so natural that we often don't even notice we're doing it.

Through my years of coaching, I've noticed how this future-focused thinking shows up in the quietest moments of our lives.

Like Maria, who shared during one of our sessions:

"I was finally sitting in my dream house – the one I'd worked so hard to buy – when I caught myself thinking, 'I'll be happy when I can renovate the kitchen.' That's when it hit me: I was doing it again, pushing away my present joy for some future moment."

Let's explore why we do this and, more importantly, how we can find our way back to the present moment where real happiness lives.

UNDERSTANDING OUR TIME-TRAVELING MINDS

You might be surprised to learn that our tendency to place happiness in the future isn't just a habit – it's actually wired into our brains. Recent research from Stanford University shows that when we imagine future happiness, our brains release small doses of dopamine, the same feel-good chemical we get from actual achievements. It's like our brains are giving us a tiny sample of future joy, just enough to keep us chasing it.

Think of it like this: Have you ever watched a child chase soap bubbles? Each time they reach for one, it floats just beyond their grasp. That's what we're doing with happiness when we push it into the future – we're chasing bubbles that keep drifting away as soon as we get close.

Let's try a quick exercise together. Take a moment to notice your surroundings right now. What small pleasures are you overlooking while your mind wanders to the future? Maybe it's the warmth of sunlight through your window, the comfort of your favorite chair, or the peaceful moment of reading these words. This simple act of noticing brings us back to where joy actually lives – right here, in this moment.

THE EXTERNAL VALIDATION TIME LOOP

Remember how we explored the trap of seeking validation from achievements and possessions in Chapter 1? This pattern often intertwines with our tendency to push happiness into the future, creating what I call the "external validation time loop."

Allow me to illustrate this connection with Alexandra's experience as a graphic designer finding herself caught in this double bind.

> ***"I was always thinking, 'Once I win that design award, then I'll feel successful,'" she explained. "When I finally won it, I felt great for about a week. But then I started thinking, 'Well, now I need to win an even bigger award next year to prove I'm still successful.' I was not only chasing external validation but also pushing my sense of worthiness into some future achievement."***

This story shows how external validation and future-focus often work together, creating a continuous cycle of seeking and postponing happiness. When we need others to validate our worth, we tend to project that validation into future achievements. And when we're focused on future happiness, we often imagine it coming through external recognition or accomplishments.

Understanding this connection helps us address both patterns together. We can ask ourselves: "Am I pushing happiness into the future because I'm waiting for external validation? What would it feel like to accept and appreciate myself right now, in this moment?"

BREAKING FREE FROM FUTURE-FOCUS

The good news is that we can learn to find happiness in the present without giving up our dreams for the future. Think of it like learning to dance – we can move forward while still enjoying each step along the way.

> James, a creative professional I worked with, shared a beautiful insight:
> ***"I used to think appreciating the present meant settling for less. Now I understand that being happy now actually gives me more energy and clarity to create the future I want. It's like the difference between forcing a flower to bloom and nurturing it while it grows."***

Let's explore some gentle ways to shift our attention back to the present moment without losing sight of our goals:

Present Moment Check-Ins: Start by simply noticing when your mind travels to the future. Like catching yourself in a daydream, this awareness itself begins to change the pattern. Try setting a gentle reminder on your phone – not to judge yourself, but to invite your attention back to now.

Joy Spotting Practice: Throughout your day, notice small moments of pleasure or contentment. Maybe it's the first sip of morning coffee, a kind exchange with a stranger, or the satisfaction of completing a simple task. These moments are like tiny anchors, keeping us connected to present joy.

FINDING PEACE IN DEMANDING TIMES

You might be wondering, "This all sounds wonderful, but how can I possibly stay present when I'm facing multiple deadlines, family obligations, or major life changes?" This question reminds me of Rachel, a client who managed complex projects at a tech startup while raising two young children and planning a wedding. She discovered that stressful times actually offer unique opportunities for present-moment awareness.

> *"I used to think I needed at least thirty minutes of quiet meditation to practice being present," Rachel shared. "Then I realized I could find moments of presence right in the middle of chaos. While racing to meet a deadline, I would pause for just three breaths. During my daughter's tantrum, I would feel my feet on the floor. These tiny moments became my anchors."*

The key is understanding that present-moment awareness doesn't require perfect circumstances. In fact, stress and pressure can serve as powerful reminders to return to the present. Think of it like surfing – instead of fighting against the waves of stress, we can learn to ride them with awareness. This might mean:

- Taking three conscious breaths between meetings
- Feeling the sensation of water on your hands while washing dishes
- Noticing the colors and shapes around you during your commute
- Experiencing the physical sensations of emotion in your body when you're overwhelmed.

These micro-moments of presence can create islands of peace even during life's storms. They remind us that while we can't always control external circumstances, we can choose where we place our attention.

Future-Present Balance: Instead of abandoning future plans, we can hold them more lightly. When you notice yourself saying "I'll be happy when..." try adding "and I can also find joy right now by..."

Remember, this isn't about forcing yourself to stay present or judging yourself when your mind wanders to the future. It's about gently expanding your awareness to include the richness of the current moment while maintaining healthy aspirations for tomorrow.

YOUR JOURNEY TO PRESENT-MOMENT JOY

As we wrap up this chapter, I invite you to experiment with these ideas in your own life. Start small – perhaps with just one present-moment check-in each day. Notice how it feels to gently bring your attention back to now, like returning home to yourself again and again.

Remember, this journey isn't about perfection. It's about practicing a new way of being with ourselves and our lives, one moment at a time. Just as we learned in our previous chapter about external validation, true happiness often lives closer than we think – not in some distant achievement, but in our ability to open our hearts to the present moment.

In our next chapter, we'll explore another fascinating aspect of the happiness journey: our belief that perfect circumstances create lasting joy. But for now, take a moment to appreciate where you are right now. What simple pleasures are available to you in this very moment?

Remember, every step on this journey matters. Even reading these words and considering these ideas is an act of growth and self-discovery. Trust that as you practice returning to the present moment, you're developing a skill that will serve you for a lifetime.

CHAPTER THREE

EMBRACING LIFE'S BEAUTIFUL IMPERFECTIONS

Have you ever noticed how we often put our happiness on hold until everything is "just right"? Maybe you've thought, "I'll feel better once my desk is perfectly organized," or "I'll be able to relax when my home looks exactly like those magazine spreads." In our pursuit of the perfect environment, perfect relationships, or perfect circumstances, we might be missing the joy that lives in life's beautiful messiness.

As we've explored in our previous chapters, happiness isn't found in external validation or future achievements. Today, let's examine another subtle way we might be blocking our own joy: waiting for perfect conditions before allowing ourselves to be happy.

THE PERFECTION PUZZLE

Think about the last time you hosted a gathering at your home. Did you find yourself frantically cleaning areas guests would never see? Or perhaps you've delayed starting a project until you could create the "perfect" conditions for success. These moments reveal how perfectionism quietly influences our relationship with happiness.

Recent research from the University of California offers an interesting insight into this pattern. Studies show that individuals who maintain rigid standards for happiness actually experience 30% less life satisfaction than those who embrace life's natural variability. It's like we're holding an impossible measuring stick up to our experiences, and nothing quite measures up.

Let me share Anna's story. As a creative professional, she believed she needed the perfect workspace to produce her best work.

> ***"I spent months planning my ideal home office," she explains. "The perfect desk, perfect lighting, perfect organization system. But when I finally had everything exactly as I'd imagined, I realized I was still finding reasons why conditions weren't quite right to start my dream project."***

Does this resonate with your own experience? Take a moment to reflect on areas in your life where you might be waiting for perfect conditions before allowing yourself to feel happy or move forward.

UNDERSTANDING OUR PERFECTION PROTECTION

Our drive for perfect circumstances often serves as a form of protection. Dr. Kristin Neff's research reveals that perfectionism frequently masks a deeper need for control and safety. When we believe we can create perfect conditions, we feel more secure - but this security comes at the cost of present moment joy.

Consider Maria's experience in her relationships.

"I had this mental checklist of everything that needed to be perfect before I could fully open my heart," she shares. "My partner needed to say exactly the right things, respond exactly the right way, and understand me perfectly. I was so focused on what wasn't perfect that I almost missed the beautiful connection we already had."

Let's pause here and explore your own relationship with perfectionism. When do you find yourself using phrases like "perfect timing," "perfect conditions," or "perfect setup"? How might these expectations be affecting your ability to experience joy right now?

FINDING BEAUTY IN THE IMPERFECT

The Japanese concept of wabi-sabi offers us a different perspective. This ancient wisdom teaches us to find beauty in imperfection, impermanence, and incompleteness. Imagine discovering that the irregular grain in a wooden table actually creates its unique character, or that the slightly crooked smile in a family photo captures a moment of genuine joy.

Research from the Institute of Positive Psychology supports this approach. Studies show that people who appreciate imperfection report higher levels of creativity, resilience, and overall life satisfaction. It's like switching from a high-magnification lens that spots every flaw to a wider angle that captures the beauty of the whole picture.

BREAKING FREE FROM PERFECT CONDITIONS

Understanding how we personally relate to perfectionism can help us develop more effective strategies for change. You might recognize yourself as a detail-oriented perfectionist, focusing intensely on getting every small element exactly right. Or perhaps you're a big-picture perfectionist, constantly seeking the ideal overall outcome while sometimes missing the beauty in the details. Many of us actually combine both tendencies, applying different perfectionist styles in different areas of our lives.

Consider James, a detail-oriented perfectionist who manages creative projects.

"I used to spend hours adjusting font sizes by fractions of a point," he shares. "Meanwhile, I was missing deadlines and stressing my team." In contrast, Lisa, a big-picture perfectionist, would envision grand perfect outcomes but struggle with the practical steps to get there. "I wanted everything to be revolutionary," she explains, "but I was overlooking the small victories and incremental improvements that actually create sustainable change."

One common concern that emerges when we talk about releasing perfectionism is its perceived connection to productivity. Many of us worry that accepting imperfection might mean lowering our standards or reducing our effectiveness. However, research tells a different story. Studies from the Harvard Business Review show that embracing "good enough" actually increases productivity by reducing decision fatigue and freeing up mental energy for innovation.

Let's explore how this works through Michael's experience. As a software developer, he believed that every line of code needed to be perfect before moving forward.

> ***"I was stuck in endless revision cycles," he recalls. "When I learned to embrace iterative improvement instead of perfectionism, not only did my productivity increase, but my creativity flourished. I was less stressed, which meant I could see solutions more clearly and collaborate more effectively with my team."***

FINDING PEACE IN PROGRESS

Consider how a garden grows - not in perfect rows or at an even pace, but in a beautiful chaos of reaching, adapting, and flourishing. Your journey toward happiness can follow a similar path. Instead of waiting for perfect conditions, try these approaches:

Celebration Practice: Each evening, acknowledge three things you appreciated today, exactly as they were - imperfections and all.

Progress Photography: Take regular photos of your projects or spaces without trying to make them "picture perfect." Notice the beauty in the real, lived-in moments.

The Good Enough Game: Practice identifying when something is good enough to move forward, even if it's not perfect. Start with small, low-stakes situations and gradually apply this to bigger areas of life.

NAVIGATING CHALLENGING MOMENTS

Life has a way of testing our relationship with perfectionism, especially during unexpected disruptions. Consider Sarah's experience when a sudden power outage hit during her crucial client presentation. "In the past, this would have sent me into a perfectionist spiral," she shares. "Instead, I found peace in accepting what I couldn't control. We ended up having a genuine conversation by phone, which actually created a stronger connection with my client than a polished presentation might have."

Sometimes these challenges appear in our personal lives, catching us completely off guard. Take Marcus's story of how a plumbing emergency the night before hosting a holiday gathering tested his newfound appreciation for imperfection. "Water was everywhere, the repairman couldn't come until morning, and I had twenty people arriving the next day," he remembers. "But instead of letting it ruin the gathering, I chose to embrace the imperfect circumstances. We ended up having a memorable evening, sharing stories about our own home disaster experiences. The imperfection actually created more authentic connections."

These unplanned disruptions offer unique opportunities to practice finding peace amidst chaos. They remind us that life's most meaningful moments often emerge from situations we never could have perfectly planned.

Do you recall Rachel's story? She was navigating a career change while planning her wedding and found a valuable perspective, she shares.

> ***"I had this image of how everything should be perfectly aligned, but when I accepted that some things would be wonderfully imperfect, I could actually enjoy both journeys - the wedding planning and the career transition - instead of waiting for everything to be just right.."***

The key is understanding that accepting imperfection doesn't mean accepting mediocrity. Instead, it means acknowledging that genuine growth and authentic experiences often emerge from embracing life's natural flow, even when (especially when) it differs from our perfect plans.

MOVING FORWARD WITH GENTLE AWARENESS

As you move forward, remember that releasing perfectionism actually enhances your ability to create, connect, and contribute meaningfully to the world. When we free ourselves from the exhausting pursuit of perfection, we discover new energy for innovation, deeper capacity for connection, and greater resilience in facing life's inevitable uncertainties.

As we close this chapter, I invite you to consider: What would change in your life if you no longer needed circumstances to be perfect to feel happy? How might you treat yourself, your loved ones, and your goals differently?

Remember, the goal isn't to abandon care or attention to detail - it's to find balance between striving and accepting, between improving and appreciating. Just as we learned to release our need for external validation and future achievements, we can learn to embrace the beautiful imperfection of the present moment.

In our next chapter, we'll explore how our desires shape our experience of happiness. But for now, take a moment to appreciate something in your current environment exactly as it is - imperfect, incomplete, and perfectly worthy of your joy.

Remember, every step on this journey - even the wobbly ones - brings you closer to authentic happiness. Your willingness to explore these ideas, to question old patterns, and to embrace new perspectives is itself a beautiful example of perfect imperfection in action.

CHAPTER FOUR

UNDERSTANDING OUR RELATIONSHIP WITH DESIRES

Throughout our exploration of happiness myths, we've discovered how external validation doesn't bring lasting joy, how future-focused thinking keeps us from present contentment, and how perfectionism can block our appreciation of life's natural flow. Now, let's examine perhaps the most subtle and compelling myth of all: the belief that fulfilling our desires will lead to lasting happiness.

Think about something you deeply desire right now. It might be a material possession, a particular achievement, or a specific life change. Notice how this desire feels in your body - the subtle tension, the pulling sensation, the sense that happiness lies in obtaining this one thing. This experience is deeply human, and understanding it can transform our relationship with happiness itself.

THE NATURE OF DESIRES

Let's begin by understanding how desires work in our minds and hearts. Imagine standing in front of a beautiful bakery window. The sight of freshly baked treats creates an immediate desire. Once you satisfy this craving, another one soon takes its place - perhaps for a savory meal to balance the sweetness, or a walk to compensate for the indulgence. This simple example reveals something profound about the nature of desires: they operate in an endless chain, each fulfillment leading to a new wanting.

Recent neuroscience research helps explain this pattern. Dr. Kent Berridge's studies at the University of Michigan reveal that our brains process "wanting" and "liking" through different neural pathways. This separation helps explain why getting what we want doesn't always bring the satisfaction we expect. Our brain's "wanting" system can remain active even when our "liking" system is satisfied, creating what researchers call the "hedonic treadmill" of constant craving.

Consider Michelle's experience:

> ***"I spent years believing that each new achievement would finally make me feel complete. First, it was getting my dream job. Then it was buying the perfect house. Then it was finding the ideal relationship. Each time I fulfilled a desire, I felt momentarily satisfied, but soon found myself wanting something else. It was like trying to fill a bucket with a hole in the bottom."***

UNDERSTANDING THE DESIRE CYCLE

When we look closely at how desires operate in our lives, we can identify several distinct phases:

First comes recognition - we become aware of something we want. This might arise from a genuine need, social comparison, or marketing messages that create new desires we didn't previously have.

Next is anticipation - we begin to imagine how fulfilling this desire will make us feel. During this phase, our minds often engage in what psychologists call "affective forecasting," overestimating how much happiness the fulfillment will bring.

Then comes pursuit - we take actions to achieve or acquire what we want. This phase often brings its own satisfaction through the sense of purpose and progress.

Finally, we reach fulfillment - we obtain what we desired. Here's where something interesting happens. The satisfaction we feel usually differs from what we anticipated, and often fades more quickly than we expected.

This understanding helps explain why even significant achievements or acquisitions don't bring lasting happiness. But this doesn't mean desires are inherently problematic. Instead, we can learn to relate to them in a more balanced way.

THE WISDOM WITHIN DESIRES

Our desires can actually teach us important things about ourselves when we learn to listen more deeply. Behind each surface desire often lies a deeper yearning for connection, meaning, or growth. Understanding this helps us respond more wisely to our wants.

Let's explore this through Thomas's story. He had a persistent desire for increasingly expensive watches.

"I thought each new watch would finally make me feel successful," he shares. "But when I really examined this desire, I realized I was actually seeking a sense of worth and recognition. Once I understood this, I could address the real need rather than continuously buying more watches."

This insight reveals an important truth: desires aren't wrong or unhealthy by themselves. They become challenging when we mistake their fulfillment for the path to lasting happiness.

PRACTICAL WISDOM FOR WORKING WITH DESIRES

Understanding our relationship with desires allows us to develop more skillful ways of responding to them. Here are some approaches that can help:

The Pause Practice: When you notice a strong desire arising, pause to investigate it with curiosity rather than immediately seeking to fulfill it. Ask yourself: "What deeper need might this desire be pointing to?"

The Satisfaction Audit: Notice what truly brings lasting satisfaction in your life versus what provides only temporary pleasure. This awareness can help you make more conscious choices about which desires to pursue.

The Contentment Cultivation: Practice appreciating what you already have, while holding your desires lightly. This doesn't mean suppressing desires, but rather relating to them with greater wisdom and perspective.

NAVIGATING STRONG DESIRES

Sometimes desires feel particularly intense or urgent, especially in our professional lives where ambition, competition, and external measures of success can amplify our wanting. During these times, we might feel almost compelled to act immediately on our desires, whether it's pursuing a promotion, changing jobs, or chasing professional recognition.

Consider Alexandra's experience navigating intense professional desires while building her consulting practice.

"I found myself constantly comparing my business to others in my field,"

she explains.

"Every time I saw a competitor launch a new program or reach a milestone, I felt this overwhelming urge to immediately match or exceed their achievement. This reactive pattern was exhausting and kept pulling me away from my authentic path."

Through working with these intense desires, Alexandra developed what she calls her "desire dialogue" practice. When strong professional wants arise, she asks herself three questions:

1. "Is this desire aligned with my core values and genuine business vision?"
2. "Am I responding to internal wisdom or external pressure?"
3. "What would waiting 48 hours before acting cost me?"

This practice helped her develop a more measured approach to professional desires while maintaining her drive for excellence. "I still have ambitious goals," she shares, "but now they come from a place of authentic vision rather than reactive wanting."

Let's explore some specific strategies for handling moments of intense desire:

The PAUSE Method:

- Present moment awareness: Ground yourself in physical sensations
- Acknowledge the desire without judgment
- Understand the underlying need or fear
- Separate urgent from important
- Evaluate alignment with your values

Michael, a software development manager, used this method when faced with an opportunity to lead a high-profile project.

> ***"The desire to say yes was incredibly strong," he recalls. "The recognition and career advancement were tempting. But using the PAUSE method helped me recognize that taking on this project would compromise other commitments that were more aligned with my long-term vision."***

WORKING THROUGH SETBACKS

It's natural to encounter challenges when changing our relationship with desires. Let's explore common setbacks and specific strategies for handling them:

Desire Overwhelm: When multiple strong desires compete for attention, try the "Desire Sorting" practice. Write down everything you want, then categorize desires as:

- Essential to well-being
- Aligned with core values
- Reactive to external pressure
- Temporary or passing wants

This sorting helps you respond more wisely to multiple desires without feeling overwhelmed.

Resistance to Waiting: When you feel resistant to pausing before acting on desires, remember Jamie's strategy. As a creative director, she often faced intense desires to immediately implement new ideas. "I developed what I call my '24-hour desire container,'" she explains. "I give myself permission to fully feel the wanting while agreeing to wait one day before acting. This container gives my wiser self time to evaluate without fighting the desire itself."

Managing Professional FOMO: Career desires can feel particularly urgent when we see others advancing or achieving. David, a mid-career professional, developed an effective approach to managing this challenge. "I maintain what I call my 'Professional Peace Journal,'" he shares. "When I notice strong career-related desires arising, I document them along with my current accomplishments and growth. This helps me maintain perspective and make choices from wisdom rather than FOMO."

PRACTICAL EXERCISES FOR WORKING WITH STRONG DESIRES

The Three-Layer Desire Investigation:

1. Surface Layer: Write down the immediate desire (e.g., "I want that promotion")
2. Middle Layer: Explore emotions driving the desire ("I want to feel respected and valued")
3. Deep Layer: Identify core needs ("I need to know my work matters")

Weekly Desire Review: Set aside time each week to review professional and personal desires that arose. Notice patterns, triggers, and which desires led to wise actions versus reactive decisions.

The Desire Delay Practice: For non-urgent desires, experiment with different waiting periods:

- 24 hours for small decisions
- One week for medium choices
- One month for major changes

Notice how the desire evolves during these waiting periods. Does intensity increase or decrease? Do new insights emerge?

THE ROLE OF GRATITUDE

Cultivating gratitude plays a special role in working with desires. Research from the University of California, Berkeley shows that regular gratitude practice actually reduces the intensity of materialistic desires and increases overall life satisfaction. This doesn't happen because gratitude eliminates desires, but because it helps us appreciate what we already have while maintaining a healthier relationship with what we want.

Consider developing a daily gratitude practice that specifically acknowledges the fulfillment already present in your life. This creates a foundation of contentment that allows you to engage with desires more skillfully.

FINDING BALANCE

The goal isn't to eliminate desires - they're a natural part of being human. Instead, we can learn to hold them lightly, understanding their nature without letting them drive our happiness. This balance allows us to enjoy pursuing goals and experiencing pleasure while maintaining inner peace that doesn't depend on external fulfillment.

Remember that this is a practice, not a destination. Some days you'll find it easier to maintain perspective about your desires; other days they might feel more compelling. This variation is perfectly normal and part of the learning process.

MOVING FORWARD

Remember, working with desires is a skill that develops over time. Each time you pause to investigate a strong want, you're building your capacity for wise discernment. The goal isn't to eliminate professional ambition or personal desires, but to engage with them from a place of inner wisdom rather than reactive wanting.

As we conclude our exploration of happiness myths, we can see how our relationship with desires connects to the other patterns we've examined. Like external validation and perfectionism, desire fulfillment offers temporary satisfaction but not lasting happiness. Understanding this allows us to engage with life more wisely and find joy that doesn't depend on constantly getting what we want.

Take a moment now to reflect on what you've learned about your own relationship with desires. How might your experience of happiness change if you held your desires more lightly? What wisdom might your desires be offering about your deeper needs?

Remember, the journey to authentic happiness isn't about suppressing desires or denying yourself pleasure. It's about understanding the true nature of happiness and finding it in the present moment, regardless of whether current desires are fulfilled or not.

Your willingness to explore these patterns and question long-held beliefs about happiness is itself a profound act of growth. Trust that as you continue to work with these insights, your relationship with both desires and happiness will naturally evolve toward greater wisdom and peace.

WORKBOOK EXERCISES AND ASSESSMENTS

Introduction:

"Now that we've unpacked the myth that fulfilling our desires is the key to lasting happiness, you might be wondering how to apply these insights to your own life. It's one thing to understand these concepts intellectually, and quite another to live them out each day. This next section is designed to help you do just that. As we move into the workbook exercises and assessments, you'll have the opportunity to dive deeper into your own experiences, beliefs, and behaviors. Through a series of thought-provoking questions and practical challenges, we'll explore how to cultivate a happiness that is resilient, authentic, and deeply rooted in your everyday life. Let's begin this transformative journey by turning our insights into actions that can lead to profound changes in how we experience joy and fulfillment."

HAPPINESS BASELINE QUESTIONNAIRE

EXERCISE 1: HAPPINESS BASELINE QUESTIONNAIRE

Instructions: Answer the following questions by rating each statement on a scale from 1 to 5, where 1 = Strongly Disagree, 2 = Disagree, 3 = Neutral, 4 = Agree, and 5 = Strongly Agree. After completing the questions, add up your scores to see where you stand on the happiness baseline scale provided at the end.

QUESTIONS

1. I feel happiest when I achieve a significant personal or professional goal.

   Strongly Disagree   Disagree   Neutral   Agree   Strongly Agree

2. My happiness is often influenced by how my friends and family view my life choices.

   Strongly Disagree   Disagree   Neutral   Agree   Strongly Agree

3. I frequently find myself waiting for the "next big thing" to feel truly happy.

   Strongly Disagree   Disagree   Neutral   Agree   Strongly Agree

4. I believe that obtaining more money or buying new things makes me happier.

   Strongly Disagree   Disagree   Neutral   Agree   Strongly Agree

5. I feel a lasting sense of joy from my daily interactions and activities, regardless of their significance.

   Strongly Disagree   Disagree   Neutral   Agree   Strongly Agree

6. My mood improves significantly when I receive praise or recognition from others.

   Strongly Disagree   Disagree   Neutral   Agree   Strongly Agree

7. I tend to focus on what I lack rather than appreciating what I currently have.

   Strongly Disagree Disagree Neutral Agree Strongly Agree

8. I find joy in the simple pleasures of life, such as a quiet moment alone or a beautiful sunset.

   Strongly Disagree Disagree Neutral Agree Strongly Agree

9. My sense of well-being is largely dependent on reaching future goals or milestones.

   Strongly Disagree Disagree Neutral Agree Strongly Agree

10. I am able to maintain a positive outlook even when things don't go as planned.

    Strongly Disagree Disagree Neutral Agree Strongly Agree

SCORING SYSTEM

- **10-20 points**: 10-20 points: Low Dependence on External Factors; you likely have a healthy perspective on happiness with a strong internal locus of control.
- **21-35 points**: Moderate Dependence on External Factors; you may sometimes rely on external circumstances or achievements to dictate your happiness, but you also recognize and appreciate the joys of everyday life. Consider focusing more on internal sources of happiness and mindful practices.
- **36-50 points**: High Dependence on External Factors; your happiness may often be contingent upon external validation, achievements, or material possessions. It might be beneficial to explore ways to cultivate happiness from within and strengthen your internal sources of joy.

REFLECTION

After scoring, reflect on your results and think about areas where you might shift your focus from external validations to more intrinsic sources of happiness. This reflection will guide you in the subsequent exercises in the workbook to develop a more balanced and fulfilling approach to happiness.

EXERCISE 2: MAPPING YOUR DESIRE CYCLE

Purpose: To help you visualize the cyclical nature of desires—how achieving one desire leads to another, creating an endless loop that rarely brings lasting satisfaction. This exercise aims to increase awareness of this pattern and encourage reflection on how it affects your happiness.

Instructions

1. **Prepare Your Space**: Find a quiet place where you won't be disturbed. Have some paper and colored pens or pencils ready to help make the visualization more vivid and engaging.
2. **Identify Recent Desires**:
   - Think of 2-3 recent desires or goals you've had. These could be material things (like buying a new gadget), achievements (like getting a promotion), or experiential (like going on a vacation).
3. **Draw the Cycle**:
   - Draw a large rectangle on your paper. Divide this rectangle into segments like a table, one segment for each desire you've identified.
   - In each segment, do the following:
     - **Label**: Write the desire at the top of the segment.
     - **Before**: In the upper section of the segment, note your feelings and thoughts before achieving the desire. For example, anticipation, longing, or anxiety.
     - **During**: In the middle section, describe your feelings when the desire was fulfilled. Focus on the immediate emotions like joy, satisfaction, or relief.
     - **After**: In the lower section, reflect on your feelings a few weeks after the achievement. Did the satisfaction last? What new desire did it lead to?
4. **Connect the Cycle**:
   - Draw arrows from the 'After' section of each segment to the 'Before' section of the next. This will visually connect the cycle, showing how the fulfillment of one desire leads to the next.

COMPLETED EXAMPLE:

DESIRE: New Phone	**DESIRE:** New Job/Promotion	**DESIRE:** New Car
FEELINGS BEFORE: Excitement, Anticipation, Impatience, Hope, Eagerness, Motivation, Dreams	**FEELINGS BEFORE:** Ambitious, Drive, Determination, Focused, Professional growth, Vision, Motivated, Energized, Excitement of new challenges.	**FEELINGS BEFORE:** Excitement about upgrade/lifestyle change, Enthusiasm, Anticipation,
FEELINGS DURING: Joy, Satisfaction, Pride, Joy, Triumph, Relief, Accomplishment	**FEELINGS DURING:** Pride, Recognition, Accomplished, Successful, Sense of worth and capability, Confident.	**FEELINGS DURING:** New car excitement, Pride in ownership. Status satisfaction, Fresh start
FEELINGS AFTER: Contentment, Fulfillment, Peace, Gratitude Emerging: Normalization, Restlessness, Comparison, New Upgrade.	**FEELINGS AFTER:** Sense of competence, Routine establishment, Performance confidence Emerging: Higher position, better pay, new challenge	**FEELINGS AFTER:** Driving pleasure, Lifestyle enhancement, Comfort appreciation, Achievement satisfaction Emerging: Normalizing to new standard, Noticing newer models, Maintenance costs awareness, Future upgrade thoughts

Look at your completed desire cycle. Reflect on the patterns and emotions you see. Are there recurring feelings? Do new desires seem to sprout from the fulfillment of previous ones?

QUESTIONS FOR DEEPER REFLECTION:

1. What does this cycle tell you about the nature of your desires and happiness?

Write answer here

2. How might recognizing this pattern influence your approach to future desires?

Write answer here

3. Can you identify ways to break the cycle, or to find satisfaction in more sustainable ways?

Write answer here

Outcome

By the end of this exercise, you should have a clearer understanding of how your pursuit of desires forms a cycle that might not lead to lasting happiness. This visual and introspective activity aims to help you reconsider how you chase and fulfill desires, encouraging a more mindful and contented approach to life.

EXERCISE 3: GRATITUDE PRACTICE

Purpose: To cultivate an ongoing sense of gratitude, which research shows can significantly increase happiness and satisfaction with life. By focusing on the positives already present, you can enhance your emotional well-being and develop a greater appreciation for the everyday.

Instructions

1. **Prepare Your Journal**: Choose a journal or digital app where you can consistently record your entries. This will be your gratitude journal.

2. **Daily Entries**:
    - Each day, choose a consistent time that works for you, either in the morning or evening, and sit down for a few minutes to reflect on your day.
    - Write down three things that you are grateful for. These should be specific to that day to help you engage fully with the practice.
3. **Guide for Selecting Grateful Moments**:
    - **Personal Interactions**: Reflect on any positive interactions you had during the day. Perhaps a friend sent you a supportive message, or a stranger held the door open for you.
    - **Small Wins**: Did you accomplish a task that has been pending for a while? Maybe you finally organized your desk or cooked a delicious meal.
    - **Nature and Surroundings**: Consider elements of the natural world that brought you peace or joy. This might be a sunny day, a refreshing breeze, or a beautiful sunset.
    - **Simple Pleasures**: Think about small pleasures that you often take for granted. This could be the taste of your morning coffee, the comfort of your favorite chair, or the feeling of fresh sheets on your bed.
4. **Weekly Reflection**:
    - At the end of each week, review your entries and consider how the moments of gratitude impacted your overall mood for the week.
    - Write a brief summary of your reflections, focusing on any new discoveries about what brings you joy or contentment.

Example Entries:

- **Personal Interaction**: "I'm grateful for the laugh I shared with my colleague today over a silly mistake. It lightened my mood and reminded me of the importance of humor in the workplace."
- **Small Win**: "I'm grateful for completing my presentation ahead of schedule, which gave me a few extra hours to unwind and read my favorite book."
- **Nature and Surroundings**: "I'm grateful for the brief rain shower this afternoon. It was refreshing and made the whole city feel clean and vibrant."
- **Simple Pleasures**: "I'm grateful for the warm, comforting aroma of the bread I baked, filling the house and bringing a sense of coziness."

Outcome

The goal of this exercise is to shift your focus from what you perceive as missing in your life to appreciating what is present. Over time, this practice can help you develop a more positive outlook, reduce stress, and increase your overall satisfaction with life.

EXERCISE 4: DETACHMENT PRACTICE

Purpose: To develop the ability to engage in activities and pursue goals without being emotionally tied to the outcomes. This practice helps cultivate a mindset that appreciates effort and experience over specific results, reducing stress and increasing contentment.

Instructions

1. **Select an Activity**: Choose an activity that you normally feel attached to in terms of a specific outcome. This could be a work project, a personal hobby, or even a routine task.
2. **Set Intentions**:
   - Before starting the activity, consciously set an intention to focus on the process rather than the outcome. For example, "During this task, I will focus on enjoying the work I do and learning from it, regardless of the result."
3. **Engage Mindfully**:
   - Perform the activity with full awareness and presence. Pay attention to each step, noticing the sensations, thoughts, and emotions that arise.
   - If you find your mind drifting towards worries about the outcome, gently bring your focus back to the present task.
4. **Reflect After Completion**:
   - Once the activity is complete, spend a few minutes reflecting on the experience.
   - Consider the following questions:
     - How did it feel to focus on the process instead of worrying about the outcome?
     - What did you notice about your stress levels during this approach?
     - Were there aspects of the activity that you enjoyed more than usual because of this mindset?

5. **Journal Your Experience**:
    - Write down your observations in a journal. Describe what you learned about yourself and how detaching from outcomes affected your experience.
    - **Detailed Example:** For a work project, approach it by valuing collaboration and creativity, instead of fixating on the praise or recognition you might receive at the end. Notice how this shift in focus changes your engagement and reduces stress during the process.

Detailed Examples to Apply Detachment

- **Work Project**: For a work project, approach it by valuing collaboration and creativity, instead of fixating on the praise or recognition you might receive at the end. Notice how this shift in focus changes your engagement and reduces stress during the process.
- **Cooking**: Cook a meal focusing on the act of cooking—enjoy the flavors, aromas, and the process of combining ingredients—rather than worrying about whether it will turn out to be perfect.
- **Exercise**: Work out with the aim of enjoying the moment and the movement of your body, rather than obsessing over calories burned or weight lost.

Outcome:

By practicing detachment, you can find greater joy and satisfaction in the present moment, reducing anxiety related to achieving specific results. This exercise aims to help you build resilience against the pressures of outcome-focused thinking and encourage a more mindful, contented approach to life's activities.

FINAL REFLECTION:

1. How did it feel to complete this exercise?

Write answer here

2. What insights have you gained, and what can you take away from this exercise?

Write answer here

3. Going forward, how you will apply these learnings to enhance your daily happiness?

Write answer here

IN CONCLUSION

Thank you for joining me on this journey through "The Happiness Myth: Breaking Free." I hope it has inspired you to redefine happiness in more fulfilling ways.

I invite you to keep the momentum going. If you found this workbook helpful and are seeking further guidance or wish to share your experiences and breakthroughs, please feel free to connect with me. Your stories and insights not only inspire me but also help others in their journeys.

Let's Connect:

Tracey@TraceyArchambeault.com

www.TraceyArchambeault.com

MEET YOUR COACH

As a personal transformational coach, I help people get unstuck by connecting their heart and their brain, and by guiding them to discover the limiting beliefs and patterns of behavior they have used to back themselves into a corner.

TRACEY ARCHAMBEAULT

Having worked in entertainment all my life; I had mastered the art of wearing a mask and being what everyone needed me to be... always at the expense of myself. People perceived me as cool and collected, but inside I was full of turmoil and anxiety.

It was through my own journey out of attachment and scarcity that I came to realize my ability and passion for helping others. There is limitless freedom outside the box we lock ourselves into, and I want to share that with others.

I use the principles, strategies and techniques learned from my own journey to help people experience their own breakthroughs, while transforming their lives from where they are to what they truly want it to be.

Tracey

www.ingramcontent.com/pod-product-compliance
Lightning Source LLC
LaVergne TN
LVHW050924210926
848482LV00012B/531